MW00567380

I Am a Union Soldier

Diana H. Loski, D.N.

Text by Diana H. Loski
Illustrations by Kristiina W. Frost

Thomas Publications
Gettysburg, PA

Copyright © 1997 Diana H. Loski and Kristiina W. Frost

Printed and bound in the United States of America

Published by THOMAS PUBLICATIONS
          P.O. Box 3031
          Gettysburg, Pa. 17325

All rights reserved. No part of this book may be used or reproduced without written permission of the author and the publisher, except in the case of brief quotations embodied in critical essays and reviews.

ISBN-1-57747-022-2

I am a Union soldier. I fight for the North in the
American Civil War. I am an infantryman. That means
I walk everywhere and do most of the fighting.

This is my uniform. My dark blue jacket or sack coat is
made of wool. Under my jacket I wear a shirt to protect
my skin from the wool. My trousers are light blue.

My cap is called a kepi. Since I am in the infantry, a brass pin shaped like a horn is pinned or sewn on the cap.

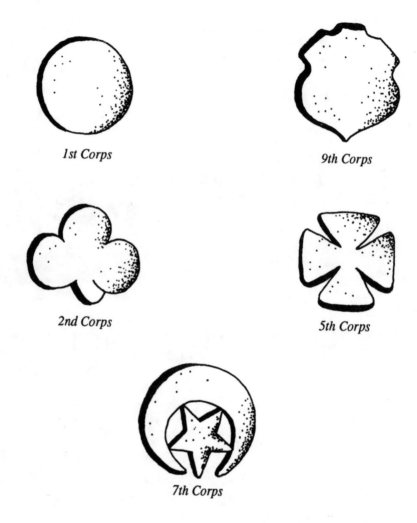

1st Corps

9th Corps

2nd Corps

5th Corps

7th Corps

Since I am in the infantry, I wear a corps emblem on my sack coat. Soldiers sometimes wear their symbol on their kepis. My emblem is the three-leaf clover, or trefoil, since I am in the Second Corps. Here are some other corps emblems.

12th & 20th Corps

3rd Corps

14th Corps

11th Corps

17th Corps

6th Corps

24th Corps

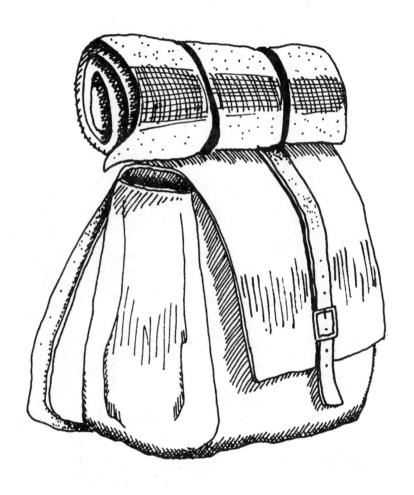

I carry with me almost everything I own. This is my
knapsack. I strap it to my back. In it I keep my extra
clothing, half of a tent, my rubber rain poncho, and
many other personal belongings. Attached to the top of
my knapsack is my blanket. I have used it to stay
warm on many cold nights.

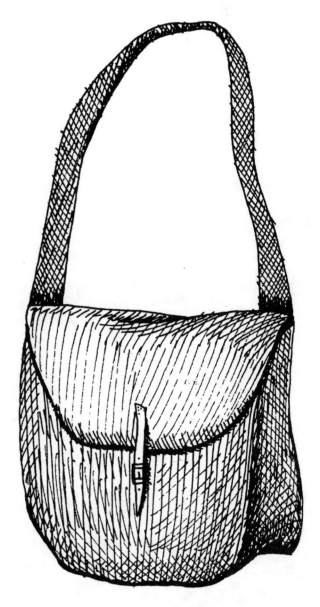

This is my haversack. It is a canvas bag where I carry my food and some personal belongings, like eating utensils, my diary, and a twist of tobacco. I carry my haversack across my shoulder.

Officers and cavalrymen wear boots. I wear leather
shoes called brogans.

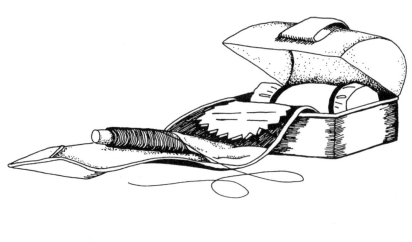

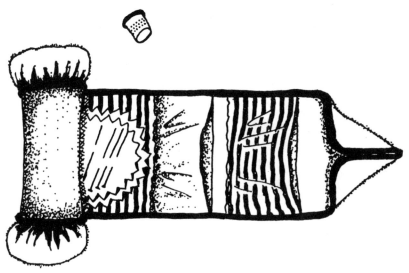

This is my sewing kit. We call it a housewife. Since our wives and mothers aren't with us to mend our clothes, we do the mending ourselves. My housewife holds a thimble, needles and thread, and scraps of cloth for patches. I keep it in my knapsack.

The food we eat most often is hardtack, a hard cracker.
We receive hardtack in five pound rations. It tastes
good when it is fresh. But by the time it reaches us it is
old and hard, almost like biting through a rock. We eat
other foods as well, like soft bread, beef and other
meats, and fruits and vegetables when we can get them.
We drink a great deal of coffee.

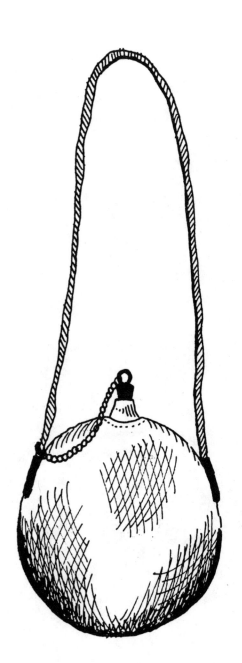

This is my canteen. It is one of my most important possessions, since it holds my drinking water. I carry it sheltered beneath my haversack, shading it from the sun.

This is my tin cup. I carry it tied to my knapsack. I use
it for drinking coffee in camp, scooping cool water from
streams, and for holding berries and nuts I gather while
foraging. Foraging means finding our own food when
there isn't any in camp.

This is my musket. I sling it over my shoulder. We attach a bayonet to the end of the musket's barrel. Bayonets look threatening because some resemble swords, but we mainly use them to dig holes when shovels are not available, to peg down our tents, and even to hold candles. Very few men have ever been wounded by the bayonet.

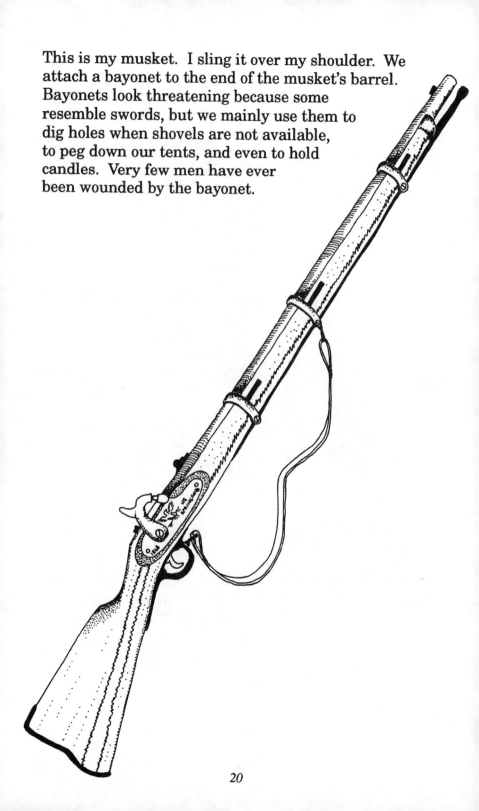

This is my cartridge box. It is made of leather and
holds my ammunition. Bullets are wrapped in paper
with a bit of black gunpowder. This makes a cartridge,
or one round of ammunition. I carry it like my
haversack, slung across my shoulder.

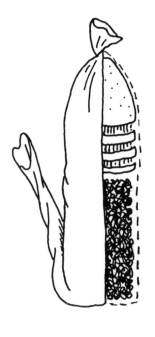

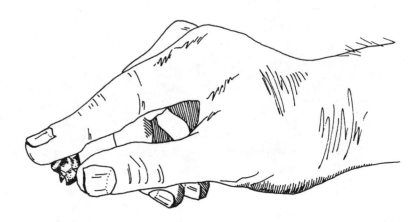

These little hat-shaped caps are called percussion caps.
I need them to fire my musket. They cause a spark to
ignite the gunpowder. I carry them in a little pouch,
attached to my belt.

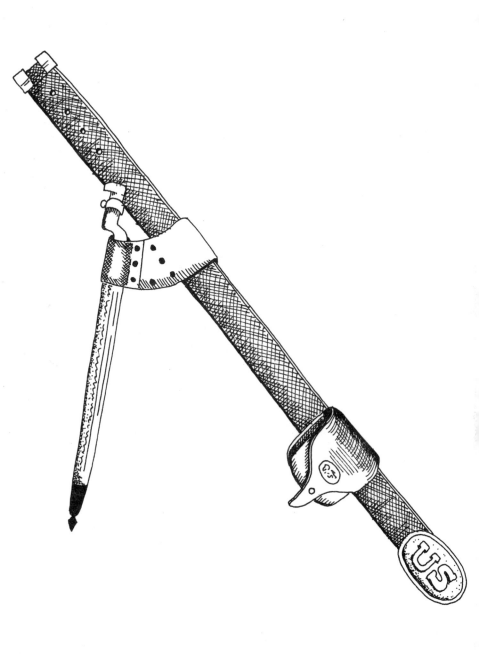

I carry my bayonet and cap pouch on my belt.

All together, my belongings weigh over twenty-five pounds. Sometimes, when we draw rations, my pack weighs even more. It gets heavy on a long march!

But, I am proud to serve my country. We carry "Old Glory" — our country's flag — wherever we go. I love our country, and our flag.

THOMAS PUBLICATIONS publishes books about the American Colonial era, the Revolutionary War, the Civil War, and other important topics. For a complete list of titles, please write to:

THOMAS PUBLICATIONS
P.O. Box 3031
Gettysburg, PA 17325